Our Mom
Is Getting Better

Alex, Emily, and Anna Rose Silver

To our mom and dad
whom we love so much

Published by the
American Cancer Society
Health Promotions
1599 Clifton Road NE
Atlanta, Georgia 30329 USA

Printed in the United States of America
5 4 3 2 1   07 08 09 10 11

Designed by Martha Benoit

Library of Congress Cataloging-in-Publication Data
Silver, Alex.
  Our mom is getting better / Alex, Emily, and Anna Rose Silver.
     p. cm.
  ISBN 978-0-944235-85-0
  1. Cancer—Chemotherapy—Juvenile literature. I. Silver, Emily. II. Silver, Anna Rose. III. Title.

  RC271.C5S525 2007
  616.99'406—dc22

                              2007014178

For more information about cancer, contact your American Cancer Society at 1-800-ACS-2345 or www.cancer.org

For bulk sales, please e-mail the American Cancer Society at **trade.sales@cancer.org**

EDITOR
Jill Russell

DIRECTOR, BOOK PUBLISHING
Len Boswell

MANAGING EDITOR
Rebecca Teaff

STRATEGIC DIRECTOR, CONTENT
Chuck Westbrook

BOOK PUBLISHING MANAGER
Candace Magee

Our Mom Is Getting Better

Alex, Emily, and Anna Rose Silver

This is a special day.
It's Mom's last session
of chemotherapy.
Chemotherapy is a kind of medicine, also
called "chemo," that makes you feel yucky,
but it helps get rid of cancer. Our mom had
cancer. But at last, after months and months
of treatment, she is finally going to be done.
We surprise her with a new watch and tell
her, "This watch means it's time to start
healing." We are all really happy about
chemotherapy ending and healing beginning.

Even though Mom has had her last chemo treatment, she isn't feeling much better yet. She is very tired all the time and tells us that she can't do a lot of things she used to do. Staying at home makes Mom feel bored, but she is still too sick to go to work. All the people at school and in our neighborhood know that Mom was sick with cancer.

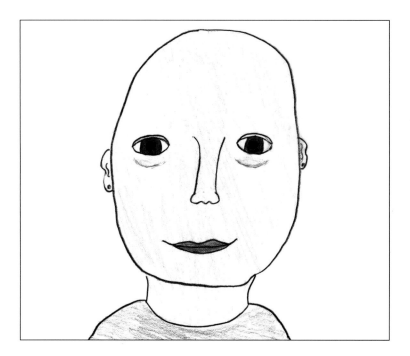

Today Mom had a checkup with the doctor. Although the worst part of the cancer treatment is over, the doctor wants her to keep taking some medicine. While Mom and Dad were gone, Grandma came over to baby-sit. We played some fun games with Grandma, but we missed Mom.

Mom's doctor tells her she should exercise more by taking walks. Mom says that we should all try to walk at least 10,000 steps every day. Now we go on lots of family walks. Mom wears a pedometer, a small machine that counts the number of steps a person takes. She is happy that everyone in the family is walking more, and she is happy that we are all getting healthier!

After Mom finished her chemotherapy, people stopped bringing us dinner. So Mom and Dad started cooking again. Mom tells us that we should try to eat lots of fruits and vegetables every day. At first, this seemed hard and we didn't like it, but now we are used to it. We like fruits better than vegetables!

It takes a long time for Mom's hair to start to grow back. After a few weeks, she begins to get some hair, but it's really short. She is still tired, so she goes to bed early. Mom goes to bed earlier than anyone else. She needs a lot of rest. Dad helps us get ready for bed, and he says that someday Mom will feel better.

"Having cancer and recovering from cancer is very stressful," Mom says. That's why she meditates every day. Sitting quietly and meditating helps Mom get rid of stress and feel better. She says that we can try meditating, too. Sometimes we try it when we are having trouble falling asleep. We know how hard cancer has been on Mom, so we are always quiet when she meditates.

Mom is starting to feel better, so she begins to take us to do some fun things. She takes us apple picking at a local farm. Our whole family goes, and it's really fun. Everyone loves picking apples. Later, when we get home, our aunt helps us bake an apple pie with the fruit we picked. It's great when Mom takes us fun places!

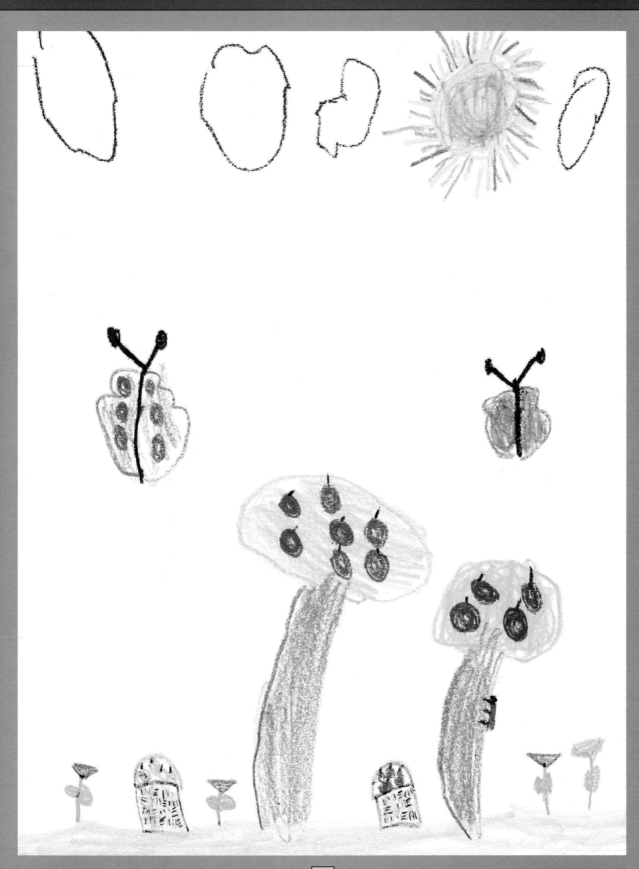

Although Mom is getting better, we still
worry that the cancer might come back.
When we ask Mom if her cancer will ever
come back, she says she doesn't think it will.
If it does, then the doctors and nurses will
help her all over again. If Mom got cancer
again, we'd be sad, but we know she would
get as much help as possible.

Today is Mom's birthday! She is feeling better, so Dad takes her out to eat at a restaurant. Mom wears a green dress and matching shoes. She wears make-up, and she looks pretty. They have a fun time talking, and the food is really good!

19

When Mom got sick, we had to cancel a family vacation we had planned with her side of the family who live far away. We all wanted to go, but we knew it would be too hard for Mom. So now that she is feeling better, we are going on a different vacation. We are happy to see our grandma, our cousins, and our aunts and uncles. We all go to an amusement park and eat popcorn and cotton candy. The rides are really fun!

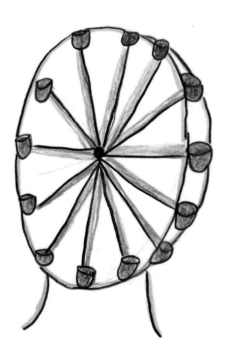

Mom says that it is time for her to go back to work. She finally feels well enough. On her first day returning to work, we all wake up early to help her get ready. Everyone agrees that this is an exciting day! Mom gives us each a big hug, and then we say goodbye as she leaves.

Our whole family wants to help raise money to cure cancer. One way we help is by walking in the Relay For Life®. Relay For Life is a wonderful event where you walk day and night around a track. People light special candles, called luminaria. Some candles make up words like "Hope."

There is also a survivors' walk, where cancer survivors like Mom walk around the track. Anyone can go to the Relay For Life—kids, families, friends—anyone. The walk raises a lot of money to help people with cancer, and it's fun to do!

It's another special day! This marks the one-year anniversary of when Mom was diagnosed with cancer. We celebrate by baking her a cake and having ice cream for dessert. Mom is still healing, but has come a long way since she got sick and is almost totally better.

Mom tells us that cancer is a terrible disease, and it hurts people a lot. But she also says that people who have had cancer can recover. This means that their lives go back to how they were before—almost. She says that life is never exactly the same after cancer, but we can still be happy!

Mom has shown us that it might be difficult at times to recover from cancer, but you can get through it. Our mom had a really big problem, but now she is feeling much better. We are all really happy that our mom is getting better!

About the Authors

Alex, Emily, and Anna Rose Silver live near Boston,
Massachusetts. Emily and Anna Rose drew the illustrations
for this book, and Alex wrote most of the text. Emily and
Anna Rose also helped write the book. Their mom is a
doctor and a cancer survivor. The Silver kids are grateful
for the opportunity to share their cancer experience with
other families.